All Kinds of Weather

Snowy Weather

A 4D BOOK

by Sally Lee

D1404596

PEBBLE
a capstone imprint

Download the Capstone 4D app!

- Ask an adult to download the Capstone 4D app.
- Scan the cover and stars inside the book for additional content.

When you scan a spread, you'll find fun extra stuff to go with this book! You can also find these things on the web at www.capstone4D.com using the password: snowy.01860

Little Pebble is published by Pebble
1710 Roe Crest Drive, North Mankato,
Minnesota 56003
www.mycapstone.com

Library of Congress Cataloging-in-Publication Data
is available on the Library of Congress website.

ISBN 978-1-9771-0186-0 (library binding)
ISBN 978-1-9771-0193-8 (paperback)
ISBN 978-1-9771-0199-0 (ebook pdf)

Editorial Credits
Marissa Kirkman, editor; Bobbie Nuytten, designer; Tracy Cummins, media researcher; Kris Wilfahrt, production specialist

Photo Credits
Getty Images: Blend Images/Jose Luis Pelaez Inc, 1; iStockphoto: FatCamera, 21; Science Source: Pekka Parviainen, 7, Ted Kinsman, 9; Shutterstock: Bogdan Hosu, 11, goodluz, 13, jonson, 5, Khrushchev Georgy, 15, Milenne Todorova, 19, Nadezda Razvodovska, Design Element, XiXinXing, 17, ysuel, Cover.

Printed and bound in the United States.
PA021

Table of Contents

Bright White

Flakes swirl in the air.

The ground is covered in white.

It's snowing.

Making Snow

Snow is made in
freezing clouds.

Ice forms on bits of dust.

These bits of frozen water
are ice crystals.
More water freezes on them.
They get bigger.

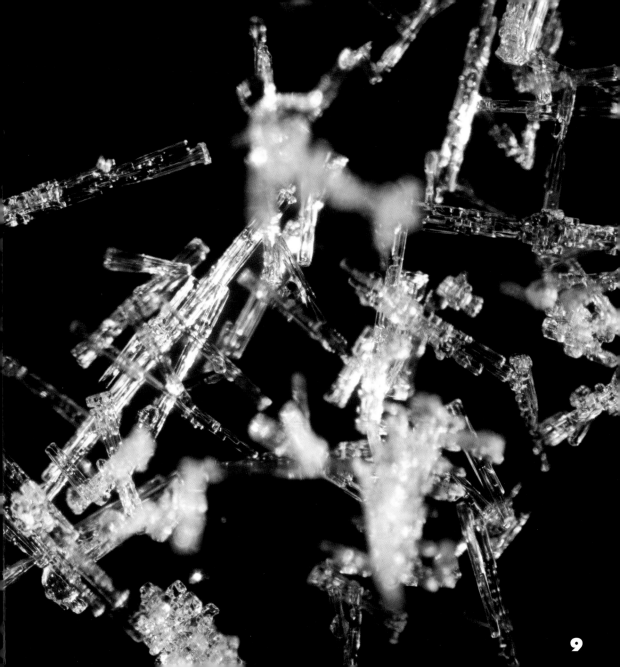

Many crystals join together.

They make snowflakes.

Each flake is different.

Snowflakes fall to the ground.

They pile on top of each other.

The snow piles are deep.

Wet or Dry?

Snow is wet in cool air.

It has more water in it.

Snow in very cold air is dry.

It has more ice in it.

Wet snow sticks together.

You can make a snowman.

Dry snow is like powder.

It doesn't stick together.

It blows out of your hands.

Have Fun!

It's a snowy day.

Grab your sled.

Zoom down a hill.

Wheee!

Glossary

dust—tiny, dry pieces of dirt or other material that is in the air

freeze—to become solid or icy at a very low temperature

ice—frozen water; water can be a solid, a liquid, or a gas; ice is a solid

ice crystal—a tiny frozen water droplet

powder—a material made up of small, fine particles

snowflake—a flake or crystal of snow; many ice crystals are clumped together in a single snowflake

Read More

Shaw, Gina. *Curious About Snow.* Smithsonian. New York: Grosset & Dunlap, 2016.

Rivera, Andrea. *Snow.* In the Sky. Minneapolis: Abdo Zoom, 2017.

Rustad, Martha E. H. *Today Is a Snowy Day.* What Is the Weather Today? North Mankato, Minn.: Capstone Press, 2017.

Internet Sites

Use FactHound to find Internet sites related to this book.

Visit www.facthound.com

Just type in 9781977101860 and go.

Super-cool stuff!

Check out projects, games and lots more at
www.capstonekids.com

Critical Thinking Questions

1. How are snowflakes made?

2. What causes a snow pile to become deep?

3. In what ways can snow be different?

Index